Hold Your Horses!

(And Other Peculiar Sayings)

written by Cynthia Amoroso ★ illustrated by Mernie Gallagher-Cole

ABOUT THE AUTHOR

As a high school English teacher and as an elementary teacher, Cynthia Amoroso has shared her love of language with students. She has always been fascinated with idioms and figures of speech. Today Cynthia is a school district administrator in Minnesota. She has two daughters who also share her love of language through reading, writing, and talking!

ABOUT THE ILLUSTRATOR

Mernie Gallagher-Cole lives in Pennsylvania with her husband and two children. She uses sayings and phrases like the ones in this book every day. She has illustrated many children's books, including *Messy Molly* and *Día De Los Muertos* for The Child's World®.

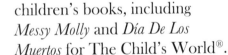

The Child's World®

Published by The Child's World®
1980 Lookout Drive • Mankato, MN 56003-1705
800-599-READ • www.childsworld.com

ACKNOWLEDGMENTS
The Child's World®: Mary Berendes,
Publishing Director

The Design Lab: Kathleen Petelinsek,
Design and Page Production

**LIBRARY OF CONGRESS
CATALOGING-IN-PUBLICATION DATA**
Amoroso, Cynthia.
  Hold your horses! (and other peculiar sayings) / by Cynthia Amoroso ; Illustrated by Mernie Gallagher-Cole.
       p. cm.
  ISBN 978-1-60253-681-4 (library bound : alk. paper)
  1. English language—Idioms—Juvenile literature.
  2. Figures of speech—Juvenile literature. 3. Clichés—Juvenile literature. I. Gallagher-Cole, Mernie.
  PE1460.A583 2011
  428.1—dc22   2010042724

Printed in the United States of America
Mankato, MN
December, 2010
PA02067

People use idioms (ID-ee-umz) every day. These are sayings and phrases with meanings that are different from the actual words. Some idioms seem silly. Many of them don't make much sense . . . at first.

This book will help you understand some of the most common idioms. It will tell you how you might hear a saying or phrase. It will tell you what the saying really means. All of these sayings and short phrases—even the silly ones—are an important part of our language!

TABLE *of* CONTENTS

As the crow flies

Caleb stared out the window as Grandpa drove down the highway. They were heading toward the mountains, and Caleb was excited.

"How far away are the mountains, Grandpa?" asked Caleb.

"They're about 50 miles as the crow flies," said Grandpa, "but it's farther by car. The road winds around a lot."

MEANING: A straight line from one place to another

Better safe than sorry

Jonathan's family was getting ready to go to a football game. Jonathan opened the front door and quickly shut it again. "Brrrr!" he said. "It's cold outside!"

His dad nodded and said, "I think it might rain, too. We better take our rain gear."

"But we'll have to carry everything," Jonathan protested. "It's a long walk from the car."

"I know," said Dad. "But if we get wet, we'll be way too cold. Better safe than sorry!"

MEANING: Be cautious; avoid obvious risks

Burn the candle at both ends

Sadie was worried about her older sister, Kate. Usually Kate was cheerful and fun. But lately she seemed cranky and tired.

"Kate's just busy right now," explained Sadie's mom. "She's getting used to her new job, and she's still taking classes at night. She's really burning the candle at both ends! I'm sure she'll feel better once her classes are done."

MEANING: To work too hard at too many things

Change of heart

"Hey, Molly!" called Kelsey. "Come and see our new puppy! His name is Shadow."

Molly ran to Kelsey's yard and saw a black and white ball of fluff.

"He's adorable!" Molly said. "But I thought your mom said you couldn't get a puppy."

"She did," answered Kelsey. "But when she saw how well I took care of the neighbors' dog last month, she had a change of heart."

Meaning: To change your feelings or attitude about something

Child's play

Michael and his Uncle Ethan loved to go on bike rides together. But this week, Michael had some bad news. "My wheel is bent," he told his uncle. "It wobbles when I ride it. I don't know how to fix a bent wheel."

"It seems pretty hard, doesn't it?" said Uncle Ethan. "But with the right tools, it's child's play! I'll bring my spoke wrench and show you how."

MEANING: Something simple or very easy

The coast is clear

Sarah and her mom were planning a birthday surprise for Sarah's dad. They were going to hide some new fishing gear in his study. When he came in, he would get a big surprise! But first they had to sneak everything into the house.

"Where is he?" asked Sarah in a whisper. "I'll carry it inside when he can't see me."

"He just went out back," replied Mom. "Go ahead—the coast is clear!"

MEANING: There is no danger; no one will see you

Easier said than done

Jenna and some buddies were playing softball against Jenna's sister and her friends. It was the first inning, and Jenna's team was already behind. Jenna was next at bat.

"Come on, Jenna!" yelled her best friend, Britta. "Make it a home run!"

"Easier said than done!" Jenna said with a smile. "Have you seen my sister pitch?"

MEANING: Something is harder to do than to talk about

Fit to be tied

Jaden loved to spend time with Grandpa. Grandpa told great stories about when Jaden's dad was little. Sometimes Dad had been pretty naughty!

"Did he really break a window?" asked Jaden.

"He sure did!" answered Grandpa with a chuckle. "And it was a big one, too. He was supposed to be using his plastic bat and ball, but he used a real baseball instead. I was fit to be tied!"

MEANING: To be angry or upset

Get in on the ground floor

Devon's mom was excited about her new job. She was working for a company that had just started up. So far, only three people worked there. The owner planned to hire more people in a few months.

"Isn't it a lot of work in the meantime?" asked Devon.

"It sure is," Mom replied, "but it's worth it. This way, I'm getting in on the ground floor. As the company grows, my job will grow, too!"

MEANING: To start something; to be involved in something from the beginning

Get your act together

Jenny's sister Mia always visited with friends after school. Lately, however, she came home right away and went straight to her room. Whenever Jenny peeked in the door, Mia was doing homework.

"What's going on?" she asked Mia. "Don't you like to be with your friends anymore?"

"Of course I do," answered Mia, "but my grades have been slipping. Mrs. Alfred told me that I have to get my act together if I want to apply for that scholarship!"

MEANING: To get organized; to be more effective

Go for broke

Alex was a good runner, and a careful one. He held back a little in races so he would have a strong finish. Today, he was running against a long-time rival. He didn't want to lose this race! When the starting gun fired, Alex took off and left the other runner far behind.

"That was amazing!" said his coach after the race. "I've never seen you run like that."

"I know," said Alex with a grin. "I decided it was time to go for broke."

MEANING: To take risks in order to win; to give something your best effort.

Happy-go-lucky

Josh's Uncle Rob lived far away, and Josh had never met him. Now Uncle Rob was coming to visit. Josh was excited. He asked his parents what Uncle Rob was like.

"He's very nice," Mom said. "He never gets discouraged or upset. If something goes wrong, he shakes it off and keeps going."

"That's true," said Dad. "He's really a happy-go-lucky guy."

MEANING: To be cheerful, happy; to not worry about things.

Hold your horses

"Can we go and sing to Mom now?" asked Emma.

"Not yet," Dad replied. "Let's get Mom's present wrapped first. And let's butter her toast, or it won't be much of a breakfast in bed!"

"But I don't want her to get up before we start singing!" said Emma.

"Hold your horses, Emma!" said Dad. "We'll be ready in just a few minutes."

MEANING: Relax, calm down, wait

In the doghouse

Tyra and Annie were playing kickball in the yard. Tyra gave a big kick, and the ball sailed right into Mom's flowerbed. Both girls ran to look.

"Uh-oh!" said Annie. "Mom's new plants are squashed flat."

"They sure are," said Tyra. "I'll be in the doghouse now!"

MEANING: In trouble

Leave no stone unturned

Maddie's cat wasn't feeling well. She and her dad took the cat to Dr. Brunswick, the vet. Dr. Brunswick examined the cat and asked lots of questions, but couldn't find anything wrong. He suggested running some tests. Maddie's dad agreed. Then Dr. Brunswick turned to Maddie. "You look worried," he said.

Maddie nodded. "I'm afraid you won't figure out what's wrong," she said.

"Don't worry about that," said Dr. Brunswick. "We'll leave no stone unturned."

MEANING: To be thorough in doing something

The lion's share

Justin and his older brother Wyatt earned money by doing chores for neighbors. They had just done some yard work at two different houses. They brought their money home and counted it out on the table.

"Hey," said their sister Abby as she watched, "it looks as though Wyatt got the lion's share of the money!"

"That's OK," said Justin. "He also did the lion's share of the work!"

MEANING: The larger share or portion of something

Mark my words

Rachel was determined to improve her standing on the tennis team. She practiced and practiced.

"She's doing great," said the coach to Rachel's mom. "She listens well, and she really works hard. Mark my words if she keeps this up all season, she'll end up being our top player."

MEANING: Remember that I told you this; I'm predicting this is going to happen

Neck of the woods

Lauren and her family were on vacation at the beach. Lauren made friends with a really nice girl named Paige. Now both families were leaving for home. It was time to say goodbye, and the girls were feeling sad.

Lauren's dad walked over to Paige's parents. "Let's stay in touch," he said. "Here's our phone number. The next time you're in our neck of the woods, give us a call so the girls can get together."

MEANING: An area or neighborhood

No skin off my nose

Alex had her glitter and glue ready. She set the poster paper on the floor of her room. She couldn't wait to get started on her project. The more glitter, the better!

"You aren't doing this here, are you?" asked Belinda. "Mom will be mad if you get glue on the carpet."

Alex shrugged. "I'll be careful," she said.

"Fine," said Belinda. "It's your room. If you get in trouble, it's no skin off my nose!"

MEANING: It's no concern of mine; the outcome doesn't affect me

Off the hook

Ian woke up worried. He had practiced his spelling words last night, but he was still having trouble. He could finish learning them if he had more time, but the test was first thing this morning!

His mom came into the room and opened the blinds. Everything outside was a dazzling white.

"Guess what?" she said. "We had 9 inches of snow last night and there is no school today. You're off the hook!" She smiled and added, "Until tomorrow, anyway."

MEANING: To get out of an unpleasant situation or an unpleasant duty

On the house

Today was Ashley's twelfth birthday. Her grandparents took her out for dinner.

"What do they have for dessert?" Ashley asked when they were done.

Before her grandparents could answer, the server walked up to their table. He was carrying a big piece of chocolate cake. Ashley's eyes lit up.

"We heard it's your birthday," the server said. "Here's your birthday dessert. It's on the house!"

MEANING: To receive something for free instead of paying for it

Pack it in

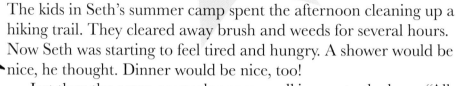

The kids in Seth's summer camp spent the afternoon cleaning up a hiking trail. They cleared away brush and weeds for several hours. Now Seth was starting to feel tired and hungry. A shower would be nice, he thought. Dinner would be nice, too!

Just then the camp counselor came walking up to the boys. "All right, guys," he said. "Let's pack it in. You've done a lot, and there's dinner waiting back at camp."

MEANING: To stop doing something

Piece of cake

Zeke was teaching his cousin Daniel some magic tricks. Daniel watched in delight as Zeke moved his fingers and made a quarter disappear.

"Wow," Daniel said. "I don't think I can do that."

"Sure you can," Zeke said. "Once you learn the secret, it's a piece of cake."

MEANING: Something that is very easy

Pull it off

Rehearsals were almost over, and the school play was going well. Then the night before the performance, the lead actor got sick. His understudy, Dillon, got ready to take his place. Dillon was nervous. So was everyone else. How would they do without their best actor?

The performance was great! Afterward, Dillon talked to the director.

"I wasn't sure we could do it," said Dillon with a big smile, "but we pulled it off!"

MEANING: To make something happen, especially if it's something you didn't think you could do

Put your foot in your mouth

Matthew thought Clara was really cute. He worried that if his buddies knew that he liked her, they would tease him.

"I think you like Clara," said Seth in the lunchroom. "I bet you'd like to ask her out."

"No way," said Matthew. "I wouldn't ask her out if she was the last girl in school!"

"That's too bad," said Seth, "because she's right behind you!"

Matthew turned around, and there was Clara! She looked mad, too.

"Oh no," thought Matthew. "I really put my foot in my mouth this time!"

MEANING: To say the wrong thing; to say something you shouldn't

Red carpet treatment

Nick's grandpa had been in the hospital for weeks. He was finally coming home.

Nick and his Dad picked him up from the hospital. When they got home, a whole crowd was waiting. Nick's mom, his sisters, and a lot of neighbors were there. Some of them had balloons and signs.

"Wow!" said Grandpa. "This is really nice. I wasn't expecting the red carpet treatment!"

MEANING: To treat someone specially; to treat someone like a celebrity

Rule the roost

Dominic liked to visit his neighbors. Mr. and Mrs. Monroe had a cat and three big dogs. Dominic was in their kitchen, eating a cookie. The three dogs were sleeping by a big water dish.

Suddenly a small black cat walked into the kitchen and headed toward the dish. The cat arched her back and hissed. The dogs scrambled to their feet and hurried out of the room.

Mr. Monroe laughed. "Well, we certainly know who rules the roost!" he said.

MEANING: To be the boss; to be in charge of something

Sit tight

Mom was driving Bella and her big brother to the movies.

"We have to make a stop on the way," Mom explained. "I have to mail this package. We have just enough time."

She pulled into a parking space, grabbed the package, and picked up her purse.

"You kids sit tight," she said. "I'll be right back."

MEANING: To be patient; to wait